# HIT-GIRL

**KICK-ASS 2 PRELUDE: HIT-GIRL.** Contains material originally published in magazine form as HIT-GIRL #1-5. First printing 2013. ISBN# 978-0-7851-6598-9. Published by MARVEL WORLDWIDE, INC., a subsidiary of MARVEL ENTERTAINMENT, LLC. OFFICE OF PUBLICATION: 135 West 50th Street, New York, NY 10020. Copyright © 2012 and 2013 Millarworld Limited and John S. Romita. All rights reserved. HIT-GIRL, KICK-ASS, KICK-ASS 2 and the Hit-Girl, Kick-Ass and Kick-Ass 2 logos, and all characters and content herein and the likenesses thereof are trademarks of Millarworld Limited and John S. Romita, unless otherwise expressly noted. The events and characters presented are intended as fiction. Any similarity to real events or to persons living or dead is purely coincidental. This work may not be reproduced, except in small amounts for journalistic or review purposes, without permission of the authors. ICON and the Icon logo are trademarks of Marvel Characters, Inc. MILLARWORLD and the Millarworld logo are trademarks of Millarworld Limited. **Printed in the U.S.A** ALAN FINE, EVP - Office of the President, Marvel Worldwide, Inc. and EVP & CMO Marvel Characters B.V.; DAN BUCKLEY, Publisher & President - Print, Animation & Digital Divisions; JOE QUESADA, Chief Creative Officer; TOM BREVOORT, SVP of Publishing; DAVID BOGART, SVP of Operations & Procurement, Publishing; C.B. CEBULSKI, SVP of Creator & Content Development; DAVID GABRIEL, SVP of Print & Digital Publishing Sales; JIM O'KEEFE, VP of Operations & Logistics; DAN CARR, Executive Director of Publishing Technology; SUSAN CRESPI, Editorial Operations Manager; ALEX MORALES, Publishing Operations Manager; STAN LEE, Chairman Emeritus. For information regarding advertising in Marvel Comics or on Marvel.com, please contact Niza Disla, Director of Marvel Partnerships, at ndisla@marvel.com. For Marvel subscription inquiries, please call 800-217-9158. **Manufactured between**

# HIT-GIRL

Writer & Co-Creator
## MARK MILLAR

Breakdowns & Co-Creator
## JOHN ROMITA JR.

Finishes & Ink Washes
### TOM PALMER

Colorist
### DEAN WHITE
with MICHAEL KELLEHER

Letterer
## CHRIS ELIOPOULOS

Editor
## JENNIFER LEE

Collection Editor **JENNIFER LEE**

Book Designer **SPRING HOTELING**

SVP of Print & Digital Publishing Sales **DAVID GABRIEL**

SVP of Operations & Procurement, Publishing **DAVID BOGART**

I am writing this to you from Mark Millar's dank, Scottish cellar. He says if I don't keep typing, he's going to turn on those jumper cables he's got hooked up to my balls! He went for a pint though, so please, I have seconds, seconds only! Someone send help! Please, I hear him coming bac—

ZZZttt!!!

Aagh!!

So, maybe that's not exactly true. Maybe I'm actually writing this from the comfort of my desk in Long Island. But you'd believe it, right? It's exactly the sort of thing you expect from a man who's written more gut-wrenching ultraviolence, more earth-shaking action than anyone I know. Hell, it's the kind of thing I expected, too, when I first met him.

Which brings me to London, spring 2012. I was there for my first Kapow!Con, and I had barely dropped off my bags when I got a text from Mark, asking me to come meet him for a drink. We had chatted through emails a bit in the weeks leading up to the convention, but I'd never met the man face-to-face. I was nervous. I half expected to walk up to the convention center and see some douchebag come flying through the glass, Mark stepping out after him, swords strapped on, pint in hand, delivering some awesome quip in a growling brogue before chopping the guy's feet off.

But that's not the man I found sitting there at the café by the convention offices. The man I found, Mark Millar, was cradling and feeding his newborn daughter, sipping at a coffee. As soon as he saw me he smiled and waved me over. "Young man!" he said, offering me a seat.

You can probably guess this initial meeting didn't end with the death of untold hundreds. It was really just a great conversation. I have young children myself, and so we got lost for a while, trading stories about these beautiful kids who keep us up all night like fucking maniacs, but whom we love more than the world. Honestly, it surprised me a little, how open and down-to-earth Mark was from go, and above all, how heartfelt his conversation was. Thinking back now, though, I know it shouldn't have surprised me. Because the ugly truth is that at its core, for me, Mark's work has always been about heart.

Now I can hear you out there: "Heart? Fuck off Snyder!" But hear me out…

Because for me, what makes Mark's work beloved by fans around the world isn't really the ball-zapping thrills or the incredible action. It's his love for his characters. It's the way he makes you relate to and care deeply about each of his creations from the first turn of the page. The craftsmanship in each voice, the quirks in each character's thinking—Mark makes his characters' hearts beat for you, makes them live for you in the most immediate, gripping ways. Better than just about anyone. So at the risk of offending you guys (and maybe even you, Mark), I'd say that at the very heart of Mark's work is, well… heart. Yes, this book has the hyper-violent awesomeness you want and expect from Mark (wait 'til you get to the teddy-bear execution!)... but the magic of the book is how Mark brings to life Mindy's everyday problems side-by-side with the badassery. Here, in HIT-GIRL, we see her vulnerable for the first time, really vulnerable. Don't get me wrong, this is the Mindy you know and love—the vigilante, raised to be the toughest, deadliest hero in the world. But it's also Mindy the kid, trying to figure out how to be child, a daughter, a friend... a Mindy I'm sure you'll come to know and love even more.

Now if Mark's writing is the heart of this book, then John Romita Jr.'s storytelling is its soul. After all, what awesome thing is there to say about his work that hasn't been said before? His signature style is here in all its glory, so expressive and dynamic. His storytelling has never been better than it is in HIT-GIRL. And of course, here there's an extra thrill of getting to see him cut loose, shake off the restraints of all things kid-friendly, and get totally down and dirty. You can just tell from the art how much fun he's having, and it makes for an incredible read. And there's no overestimating the contribution of the crew John has with him here. Between Tom Palmer's rich line-work and finishes, Dean White's evocative colors and Chris Eliopoulos' artful lettering, you've got one of the best teams in visual storytelling.

So friends, to finish up, what follows here is a great book, by a great team, featuring the most bad-ass character currently in comics... There's no way you can read this book and not get swept away by the characters, the mindblowing action, and the adoration of comics inherent on every page. Because, like all the KICK-ASS books, this one is also about the transformative power of comics, about their ability to inspire wonder and desires—good and bad. Like I said, it's a book made with much love, and I couldn't be more honored that Mark decided to reach out to me to write this. Savor this book; it's a wonder.

Still, the next time Mark invites me for a drink, he better bring his fucking swords. Swords, Mark!

*Scott Snyder is a novelist and the award-winning writer for BATMAN, SWAMP THING, SEVERED, and AMERICAN VAMPIRE.*

Six months ago, my days would have started with a meat smoothie and a hundred chin-ups.

Mornings could be anything from stunt-driving to knife throwing, afternoons usually written exercises like fingerprint analysis or C.I.A. torture techniques.

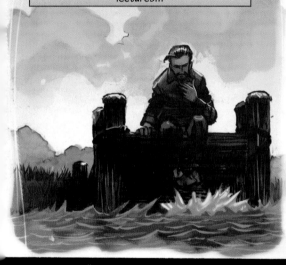

One time Dad handcuffed my hands behind my back and tossed me in the river to see if I'd been paying attention to his *escapology* lectures...

How we *doing* down there, Mindy? Everything *hunky-dory*?

A superhero needs to [be] *resourceful*, honey-b[un]. You never know *what* t[he] bad guys are gonna hit us with.

...and he was *absolutely right*.

How do I *look?*

Like a *million dollars.*

You ready to go *fishing,* Kick-Ass?

*Fuck* yeah.

My dad and I used to do this all the time. The idea's just like *real* fishing except Dad and me used *bling* instead of bait.

What's cool is that this doesn't just hone a superhero's *street-fighting* skills. This part of town is an open sewer so it also doubles up as a *cleansing operation.*

**Kick-Ass, this is Hit-Girl. I just drugged Mom and Marcus and I'm heading for the Hit-Car now. I'll pick you up in *twenty minutes*. Do you copy?**

**No problemo...**

**...I'm just writing an article for CBR on how few super heroes have been created in the last forty years compared to the *previous* four decades.**

**They really liked that piece I did on Vertigo's paper stock and said I could have another 2,000 words.**

**Dave, *listen* to me. I don't *give* a shit. You're going to be up against *Russians* and *Sicilians* here, so I want you to give this your *full attention*.**

**I want you in costume in *twenty minutes*.**

**Okay, okay. I'm on my *way*, Ms. Bossypants.**

Attaboy, Kick-Ass! You're doing **pretty good**.

Put down as many as you **can**. I got your back...

UNG!

What the hell?

Are you okay?

I-I'm fine. I just...

THAT GUY JUST SHOT OUR DAD!

What?

It's okay! I got him!

Get off me, you idiot!

What the hell? Were you just watching me use the *bathroom,* you lesbian?

"Wake up, bitch.

"C'mon. I didn't haul your ass up here so you could take a *nap.*"

Wh-What?

Wh-Where am I? I...

**Mindy's House:**

Hey, honey. What's up?

You *lied* to me, Marcus. You said they weren't *leaning* on you, but look what just got delivered. It says *Mommy Bear*, *Daddy Bear* and *Baby Bear* on them...

Oh, Jesus.

**The Police Department:**

Gigante, I need to *talk* to you.

But the cops don't want to know. Not as long as they're getting their kickback from UNCLE GODDAMN RALPHIE.

I planned to tie the exits shut and torch the entire building, but I didn't count on so many GIRLS working here.

Some of them don't look much older than ME.

Hey, Rudy. Go get us another bottle.

Whatever you say, Spoons.

Guess I should be sensible and head outside.

Wait for them across the street and pick them off with my sniper rifle before anyone even...

Eight different HEAVIES in his inner circle. All well-built and armed to the teeth.

Why the hell did you have to stand me up TONIGHT, Kick-Ass?

**Marcus? everything okay?**

**Huh?**

Oh, hey, honey. I just got in two minutes ago and heard Mindy *shouting.* She must have been having a nightmare.

Yeah, I guess I must have been having a bad dream or something, Mom. Is it time to get up for *school?*

No, not for another half hour. Come to bed and cuddle for a while, Marcus. The alarm won't go off until 7 a.m.

No problem, sweetheart.

Do you realize what this would *do* to her? She's been freaking out about those *bullets* we got sent. Can you imagine what she'd be like if she found out you were *Hit-Girl?*

To be *continued.*

Ready?

Like you wouldn't *believe.*

Okay, boys. Let's go to work.

Marcus, this is *nuts!* It could have been *anyone* in that Hit-Girl costume. I *told* you I was *fast asleep.*

Well, I guess fifteen years in law enforcement has made me a little *cynical,* Mindy. Locks are going on the doors and windows. Just to put my mind at ease.

I've also disconnected your computer and all your comic books are going in the garage until you're *eighteen years old.*

I flicked through some of this stuff and I'm *not surprised* you've ended up with homicidal tendencies.

THE SECRET SERVICE

Oh, *man.*

But the *biggest* change I made is switching my shifts to permanent daytime. Just so I can keep *an eye* on you at night.

I've no idea how you managed to *sneak out* in the past, but I promise I will see you *in jail* before I see you do this again.

This is *unbelievable.*

I'd spent *weeks* coming up with the coolest deaths and funny little quips as I finished them off.

I crossed the city like a fucked-up Santa, sliding down chimneys and dispensing death like candy canes.

I nixed them all in a single night and don't know how I did it, but I hadn't had this much fun since Daddy gave me that *terrorist* to play with on my eighth birthday.

Strangled. Decapitated. Blown to pieces with *grenades* up their asses. It was *awesome*.

But the boss I saved for *last*. The guy who thought he was safe up there in his *big castle*.

GUARDS! GET IN HERE! THERE'S A MIDGET WITH A GUN AND SHE'S GONNA FUCKING SHOOT ME!

What the hell's going on with all this *midget* shit?

Scream all you *like*, by the way. I hit the place with *knock-out gas*. Likewise, the guys in the monitor room are busy watching last night's *security tapes*.

I've been planning this for *months* and tonight I just offed everyone you ever valued in your dirty *chain-of-command*.

Who the fuck *are* you, kid?

Oh, just a little girl who likes her *bedtime stories*. Have you heard the one about the *three bears*?

Mommy Bear, Daddy Bear...and *Baby* Bear...

MOMMA BEAR

POPPA BEAR

BABY BEAR

Mom and Marcus were still out cold when I got back home, and just like I hoped, Marcus took *the blame* for me.

He told his friends it was self-defense, and all the other cops figured he'd probably get a *medal* for defending his home against four armed intruders.

I just never expected *Mom* to be so freaked out. I never knew how *fragile* she was until I saw her shaking and crying in the middle of the garden.

But Marcus was *amazing.* He'd been helping her through her *anxiety attacks* and knew exactly what to do to get her breathing under *control.*

That's when I realized that Marcus was right and Mom could never know the truth about my Hit-Girl past.

The idea that her *husband* had taken four lives almost pushed her over the edge.

What would she do if she ever found out I had over a *hundred kills* under my utility belt?

Do you understand *why* this has to stop now?

*Relax,* Marcus. It's over. We're safe now *anyway.*

The local Mafia pulled right back, shell-shocked and disorientated.

Their leaders were gone, their soldiers in retreat and Marcus was no longer in danger now that *Genovese* had been taken down.

I hung up my cape and focused on school-work, but as rumors spread of what happened that night it had never been more *fashionable* to be out there in a pair of pantyhose.

Brand new heroes were appearing every day and the Twitter-sphere was blazing with *team-up* talk and *super-groups* and all these things I so *desperately* wanted.

But it wasn't just the *heroes* who were getting their asses organized.

Red Mist's video had gone seriously viral and every little prick with a history of self-harm suddenly had a *figurehead.*

**Kung-Fu School, Asia:**

The number of kids out there wanting to be *super-villains* is just *insane*, Chris. They're following you on Twitter now and making these *copycat* costumes.

It's like you're *the Joker* or something, man. They all think you're this total bad-ass and said they'll do anything you *want* when you're back in New York.

so looked into that dyguard thing you e talking about and e this huge *Russian* bitch lined up.

It's going to be expensive, especially if she's wearing the costume, but she has to be the most evil-looking thing I've ever *laid eyes* on, dude.

I remember who he *is.*

Uh, are you okay, Chris? You seem a little spaced-out. Are you *depressed* or just *stoned?*

What?

People always say that drugs aren't *good* for you, but it totally came back when I was just sitting here *getting high.*

I was staring at the dance floor and it all came *flooding back.* I remember Kick-Ass's *secret identity...*

# END OF BOOK TWO

**MARK MILLAR** has been one of Marvel's key writers in the 21st century. His first major contributions were *Ultimate X-Men* with Adam Kubert and *The Ultimates* with Bryan Hitch, which *Time* magazine named 2010's Best Comic Book of the Decade. His *Wolverine* and *Marvel Knights Spider-Man* runs were also best sellers, but it was his epic *Civil War* series that reshaped the Marvel Universe and remains the publisher's best-selling title of the last decade. His Millarworld company boasts a roster of creator-owned books such as *Wanted*, turned into a blockbuster movie starring Angelina Jolie; *Kick-Ass*, which starred Nicolas Cage; and *Nemesis*, with Steve McNiven. Millar's other creator-owned works include *Supercrooks* with Leinil Yu, *The Secret Service* with *Watchmen*'s Dave Gibbons, and a new superhero series with fellow Scot Frank Quitely. In his native U.K., he's the editor of *CLiNT* magazine, an advisor on film to the Scottish government, and managing director of TV company Millarworld Productions. He was recently named the creative consultant for the Marvel franchise movies developed at FOX.

**JOHN ROMITA JR** is a modern-day comic-art master, following in his legendary father's footsteps. Timeless runs on *Iron Man*, *Uncanny X-Men*, *Amazing Spider-Man,* and *Daredevil* helped establish him as his own man artistically, and his work on *Wolverine* and *World War Hulk* is arguably the most explosive comic art of the last decade. In addition to *Eternals* with writer Neil Gaiman, JRJR teamed with Mark Millar on the creator-owned *Kick-Ass*, later developed into a blockbuster feature film starring Nicolas Cage. Avid Spider-Man fans rejoiced at the artist's return to *Amazing Spider-Man* with the Brand New Day storylines "New Ways To Die" and "Character Assassination." He later joined writer Brian Michael Bendis on the relaunched *Avengers*. Recent titles include the blockbuster crossover *Avengers vs X-Men*, and the relaunch of *Captain America*.

**TOM PALMER** has worked as an illustrator in the advertising and editorial fields, but has spent the majority of his career in comic books. His first assignment, fresh out of art school, was on *Doctor Strange*. He has since gone on to lend his inking talents to many of Marvel's top titles, including *X-Men*, *The Avengers*, *Tomb of Dracula*, and more recently *Punisher*, *Hulk,* and *Ghost Rider*. He lives and works in New Jersey.

**HITE** is
e comic
s best and
ght-after
sts. Well-
r his work
such as *The
Spider-
isher, Dark
, Captain
Black
Wolverine*,
tless more,
nvelope-
endering
palette
ense of
and power
page he

**CHRIS ELIOPOULOS**
is a multiple award-
winner for his lettering,
having worked on
dozens of books during
the twenty years he's
been in the industry –
including Erik Larsen's
*Savage Dragon*, for
which he hand–
lettered the first 100
issues. Adding to his
success as a letterer,
he also publishes his
own strip *Misery Loves
Sherman*, wrote and
illustrated the popular
*Franklin Richards: Son
of a Genius* one-shots,
and wrote Marvel's
*Lockjaw and the Pet
Avengers* series.

**JENNIFER LEE** is a story
editor and producer
working across film,
comics, and prose. She's
edited for both Marvel
and DC Comics, and her
books include *Daredevil,
Black Widow, 100 Bullet
Transmetropolitan*, and
the award-winning
illustrated prose novel
*The Sandman: The
Dream Hunters*. *Hit-Girl*
marks Jenny's reunion
with Mark Millar and
John Romita Jr, whom
she edited during their
seminal run on *Wolverin*
Film credits include *True
Adolescents* starring Ma
Duplass and Melissa Led
*Small, Beautifully Moving
Parts*; *Union Square*
starring Mira Sorvino
and Tammy Blanchard;
*Arcadia* starring John
Hawkes; and *The Skelet
Twins* starring Kristen
Wiig and Bill Hader. She
lives in New York with
her husband, comics
illustrator Cliff Chiang.

VARIANT COVERS

# KICK-ASS

## MARK MILLAR
## JOHN ROMITA JR.

MARK MILLAR · JOHN ROMITA JR.

# HIT-GIRL

# THE MILLAI

# KICK-ASS 2

## MARK MILLAR
## JOHN ROMITA JR.

# WANTED

MARK MILLAR · JG JONES · PAUL MOUNTS
NOW A MAJOR MOTION PICTURE FROM
**UNIVERSAL PICTURES**
WWW.MILLARWORLD.TV

MARK MILLAR & LEINIL YU

# SUPERIOR

FROM THE
WRITER OF
**KICK-ASS**

# WORLD COLLECTION

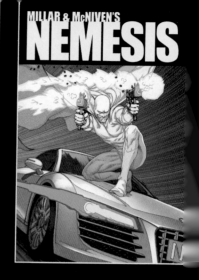

MILLAR & McNIVEN'S
## NEMESIS

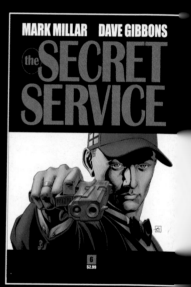

MARK MILLAR     DAVE GIBBONS
## the SECRET SERVICE

G
$2.99

MARK MILLAR · Frank Quitely
## JUPITER'S LEGACY

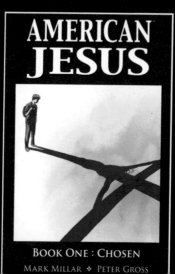

## AMERICAN JESUS

BOOK ONE : CHOSEN

MARK MILLAR ✦ Peter Gross

MARK MILLAR     LEINIL YU
## SUPER CROOKS

THE HEIST

# KICK-ASS READING ORDER

## PART ONE

## PART TWO

## PART THREE

## PART FOUR

### KICK-ASS 3

### THE GRAND FINALE

MAY 2013